The Cinder Path

poems by

Jim Garrett

Finishing Line Press
Georgetown, Kentucky

The Cinder Path

for James Burton and Adlai Marian

Copyright © 2024 by Jim Garrett
ISBN 979-8-88838-775-7 First Edition
All rights reserved under International and Pan-American Copyright Conventions. No part of this book may be reproduced in any manner whatsoever without written permission from the publisher, except in the case of brief quotations embodied in critical articles and reviews.

ACKNOWLEDGMENTS

"Foul Ball" first appeared in *Spitball: The Literary Baseball Magazine*

Publisher: Leah Huete de Maines
Editor: Christen Kincaid
Cover Photo: Marian Morton
Author Photo: Michael Starinsky
Cover Design: Elizabeth Maines McCleavy

Order online: www.finishinglinepress.com
also available on amazon.com

Author inquiries and mail orders:
Finishing Line Press
PO Box 1626
Georgetown, Kentucky 40324
USA

Contents

The Cinder Path 1
The Lighthouse at Sandy Hook 2
The Beach House, Closed 3
Closer to Shore 4
Oranges at Halftime 5
The End of the Jetty 7
To Avalon 9
Winnebago 10
Foul Ball 11
All the Way 13
My Son's Hands 14
Flashlight 15
A Boy's Armor 16
Fallen Tree 17
Exit Sandman 18
In My Father's Wake 19
My Father, Past Eighty, on the Beach 20
The Rising 21
When I Gave My Father's Eulogy 22
In the Rehab Hospital 23
Sixty Feet Six Inches 24
Wrestling with Angels 26
The Bend in the Branch 27
My Horses 28
New Neighbors on North Park 29
Shore of Home 30
Grammar of Life 31
The Corner 32
Flies and Fireflies 33
Hospice Down the Shore 34
One Night, Not Alone 35

The Cinder Path

> *The Bradford Cinder Path is a pedestrian path constructed in the 1930s that spans four blocks in Cleveland Heights, Ohio. It was designated a Cleveland Heights landmark in 2021.*

Some days I end at the beginning
Of the cinder path, looking back,
A 1930s path for children off to school
A WPA royal road of stone columns
In deep shade of ancient trees
Among new stalks of native plants
Each block another adventure
Not alone, always a chance meeting,
Neighbor, baby in stroller, friendly dog
Runner, bicyclist, doe and fawn
Count steps, stop, watch, listen
Enough quiet for my noises within
Enough relief for the grief I hold
When I end at the beginning.

Other days I begin at the end
Of the cinder path, unwinding
The time it took to get this far,
Down these doglegged blocks
Going backwards, unspooling
My life, every backward step
Not a retreat but a retrieval,
A walk back in time, eyes down,
Going back towards people I knew
Back at the beginning who once
Looked out from lighted windows
Waiting for me to return again
With something to show of my life
When I begin at the end of the path.

The Lighthouse at Sandy Hook

> *The Sandy Hook Lighthouse in Sandy Hook, New Jersey, is the oldest working lighthouse in the United States.*

Now, in the light of my I-Pad,
After heavy rain, alone, late,
Far from shore or deep sea
I see through the screen darkly

An ancient light as old as light
Rising in old mariners' eyes
In fog or storm, wind or rain
In the cold of the night

In darkness before electricity
Before Coast Guard, radar, GPS
Before the land was America
Or the harbor was Sandy Hook

The men on deck, at portholes
In cabins, starboard and port
Bow and stern and fo'c's'le
Far from shore, far from home

Keeping vigil, for the light,
A beacon out of darkness
To tell them where they are
To tell them the way to go

A welcome and a warning
For shoals, sandbars, drifts
Nor'easters, gales, squalls
A night fear of shipwreck

So I see enough by I-Pad
From out of my darkness
To write a poem about light
Alone, late, far from shore.

The Beach House, Closed

Inside the corner house
The furnace's off.
The house I love is shut
For winter, forever.

Nobody visits.
Gusts of icy wind
Rattle windows
Bang on doors.

The couch sits silent.
Beds wait for change.
Chairs huddle close
To the long table.

Silence lives alone
Inside the corner house
Where I grew up
With love.

I'd like to see that house
Alive again with people
The ones I loved and lost
Around the table.

I'd like to see them again
Who taught me about love
Awash in summer light
No end in sight.

Closer to Shore

When I was drowning
taking in gulps
kicking and sinking

closing my eyes
not seeing
the nearby pier

the idling boats
not seeing
all the life vests

when I turned away
from rescues
stared at horizons

forgot where I
was safe
almost stopped

I heard my father
ashore
in a whisper

as close to my ear
as a seashell's
roar of sea

You are closer
I heard him say
to the shore

the shore
he said
is closer to you

drowning
than you realize
swim

Oranges at Halftime

At halftime
When Mr. Bradley stood over us
Orange slices
Stuffed like candy in our mouths

We knelt
As he told us about who we were
In silence
The first half, he said, was memory

Everything now
Depended whether we were young men
Who counted
When the going was getting tougher

Then told us
To sit, relax, eat an orange, rest
Get ready
He never raised his voice

We listened
As he told us more about ourselves
Than anyone
Had ever told us in our lives

At thirteen
Huddled on grass on a Sunday afternoon
Armored
Shoulders, hips, knees, thighs, elbows

In the first half
He told us we did a lot of good
But to win
We had a lot more to do

Other people
His voice falling close to a whisper
Watched us
Not just parents and a few girlfriends

No, not
Just the crowd in the high school stands
Who counted
On us to play our best football now

But every teammate
Who played beside us every down
Every player
Who ever wore the purple and gold

And someone else
Who wasn't with us in the grass today
Or in the stands
Someone who wouldn't remember

The score
But who would remember the taste
In fifty years
Of an afternoon filled with pride

The End of the Jetty

The hottest day of the summer
Alone in the flats beside the inlet
I think I can make the end

Of the jetty for once in my life
Go, not looking back or down
Go, ahead, alone, finally go on

So I clamber between rocks
Handhold a jagged edge
Blunder down the spine

I don't stop, I don't look
Down where churlish water
Swirls, eddies, gurgles

Until, unbalanced, not halfway,
I stop. I am ten years old again
Afraid to go into the surf

As other seafaring boys
Dash headlong into waves
Throw themselves over

The swells, deep-sea divers,
While I wait, alone,
Hot feet stuck in hot sand.

Nobody sees my courage end.
Far ahead a fisherman reels.
Far behind boys plot in sand.

Before I turn back, chastened,
Hidden behind rocks ahead
Two women in chiaroscuro

Lips haloed in rising smoke
Feet dangling in the brine
A lunch break for mermaids

Who see me wavering alone.
It takes all I am to go ahead
Next step, vertigo or undertow,

Next step, the jetty a jumble
Of rock faces and lost pride
Until I totter close enough

For a hand to reach for me
And clasp my hand, and I go
All the way to the end, loved.

To Avalon

One Holy Saturday I drive
with my mother sixty years

into the past, wide highway
giving way to coastal road

time and space unspooling
moving us away from now

in the light of the years
to the beginning of time

sixty years like yesterday
a shoal rising from memory

a bridge over a marshy bay
a shore town in April light

stories of my childhood
looking for turtles in sand

her young motherhood
my father's undefeated dream:

a house by the sea, all summer,
a growing family, all gathered,

a thousand stories, a victory
every day until the day you die

my mother beside the ocean
growing younger in shore light.

Winnebago

In the summer of 1972
My father stopped time
Or at least slowed it up
For my siblings and me
The day he pulled up
In a huge Winnebago,
A king of the road,
Perched high above us
With the best news
We, 13 to 6, ever heard.
On the highway south
Down the entire coast
Through Florida groves
All my siblings dreamed
Of the Magic Kingdom,
Just opened in 1971.
I was 13, knew better,
Sitting beside him,
Unfolding a huge map
Across my knees,
Tracing the black lines
Helping find the way,
While my savvy sisters
Studied road signs
For "South of the Border"
The nearest rest stops
And my little brothers
Stared out windows
To spot some magic
As my father played
A Sinatra eight-track
Over and over again
Until the highway
and Sinatra melded
My father at the wheel
Forever forty-two
His timeless song
"Let's forget tomorrow
Tomorrow never comes!"

Foul Ball

When I was fifteen, a third baseman,
I committed three throwing errors
And struck out looking three times

While my father watched sitting alone
In grass far down the third-base line
Like a grim talent scout for the Yankees

Watching my every move at the bag
Eyeing my cuts and whiffs at the plate
Never flinching or changing the way

He looked at the game: the perfect
Dimensions of angles and lengths
Distances to throw and run and slide

And looked at me, too close to the line,
Missing a tweener too far for the shortstop
To make up the difference between us

Too far from home plate, stiff in the box,
My bat held too low, my swingless strikes,
Until I swung hard and fouled one off

My father telling me on the car ride home
It was my best swing of the game.
On top of it, he said, it didn't matter

If it was fair or foul. I had my eye on it.
My swing was level. I picked my pitch.
I hit it hard, a line drive far down

The third baseline that he had to dodge
And retrieve and return to the ump
As if he was turning in a collectible,

A home run ball, his son's walk-off homer
To win the World Series for the Bombers,
Or, as I heard in his voice driving home,

And saw in his eyes in the driveway
When he turned off the car and looked
At me, not the grim Yankees scout,

What I felt, and still feel fifty years later,
Was he so loved the game of baseball,
And wanted me to feel and know his love.

All the Way

On an early summer evening
my father sang Sinatra
as fading light found him
aglow after a spaghetti dinner
and his birthday cake
surrounded by us, sons
who looked up to his grit
and daughters who loved
his lack of it and my mother
who adored his gumption
its strength and softness
and tilting back in his chair
he crooned "All the Way"
with Sinatra's enunciation
of "When some-bod-y loves you"
his voice rising off-key
with gusto and melancholy
lingering on "Allllllllll the way"
his eyes cutting to my mother
"Deeper than the deep blue sea is
That's how deep it goes if it's real"
his head tilting towards her
"Through the good or lean years
And for all those in between years"
or "the New Orleans years"
and "all those teen years"
as I heard or wanted to hear
on that perfect summer night
us all together in an old house
by the sea at the end of time
then he stood for the finale
like Ol' Blue Eyes in his comeback
at the Main Event in the Garden
shadowboxing like a prizefighter
knocked down too many times
who gets back up again
and sings his heart out
to his adoring crowd.

My Son's Hands

In the delivery room, I watched
As the doctor held my son up
For me to see for the first time
His long skinny legs dangling
And his big hands grasping air.

When I watched his boyhood play
At first base, footwork at the bag,
Up at bat, when his big swing
Missed and missed until he got one
Clearing the bases with his slam

When I watched my son turning
the corner, his long legs and arms
In rhythm, his face grimacing
His elation and disappointment
At the finish line of the race

When I watched him on stages,
His hands deep in his pockets,
Sports dinners and graduations,
Through the door of his dorm
The day we dropped him off

I didn't see in the boy the hands
Of the husband, his big hands
Joined together with hers or
The big hands of the father
Holding a child on each knee.

Flashlight

Vermont cold in March
Late night about to go
We gave grandkids kisses,
Byes, promises to keep,
Last hugs, bedtime stories
Before our three-year-old
Still restless, wide awake
Looking for ways to delay
Our long car ride home
And terrors of bedtime
Jumped up from covers
Asked for more stories
Sorted through books
Searched under his bed
Not listening to parents
Until he scrambled up
In a dusty newsboy's cap
With a sense of purpose
Suddenly a grown boy
With a job he had to do
He pulled on a vest
Clicked on his flashlight
And led us, grandparents,
Downstairs and out
Across the dark drive
His courage and light
Showing us where
To go to find our car
And where we could
Find him, our guide,
When we returned.

A Boy's Armor

At the Cleveland Museum of Art
after running through galleries
walled with immense portraits
in gilded frames of frumpy men
around long cabinets of jewelry
glistening under tempered glass
in and out of statuary of saints
under medieval altar pieces
around marble cherubic nudes
past large idyllic landscapes
my young grandson, in awe,
at the door to the Armor Court
suddenly quit his boyishness
like Perceval beside his mother
seeing knights on horseback
riding high out of the forest
at the sight of these knights
and horses, adorned in armor,
chainmail, gauntlets, beavers
shields, swords, lances, axes
stood still, taller and older,
in front of a glass display
of a boy in armor, his own size.

Fallen Tree

Summers ago, when my son and I
walked hand in hand into woods
to a fallen tree across a worn path
we liked to think like explorers
of ways to cross to the other side
but he, just a boy, always slipped
under so easily as if born to it
while I stepped over unsteadily
his glance wary at his needy father,
a step too far, as I reached out
for his small hand to help me over.
Now, I walk with his small son,
hand in hand, two new explorers,
in search of our path, our woods,
our fallen tree, and a small boy's
chance to slip under it so easily
and when I reach out, help me too,
taking my hand to get over it,
on this long journey of finding love.

Exit Sandman

> *Hall-of-Famer Mariano Rivera pitched his last game for the Yankees on September 26, 2013.*

From his hospital bed in front of the TV
My father watches every Yankees game

Twice, live and rebroadcast, enjoying
The second time, win or lose, more

Knowing what's about to happen
The Captain up, runners on, tied

Or Sandman jogging in, last of the ninth,
The drama larger the outcome known

His hands grasp a bat he doesn't hold
When clutch Jeter steps to the plate

His fist punches his ungloved hand
When sublime Rivera delivers a strike

A Bergen County all-star catcher in '47
A semipro catcher, a '55 Pirates tryout

He bent his knees a thousand times
Face-masked, chest-protected, ready

To give the sign, check the runner's lead
Flip his mask, throw out the base stealer

And hustle every time down to first base
On every infield out or pop fly or walk

But now he lifts his knees just a little
Behind the home of his hospital bed

The final time "Enter Sandman" booms
And wakes the ghosts of Yankees past

His fingers flash the sign for Mo's cut
A heavenly pitch like Koufax's curve

His hands ready for the last pitch of all
After a hard nine innings behind the plate.

In My Father's Wake

One summer on the beach at Avalon
When as a young boy, lost in thought,
I watched my father, still a young man,
Run into the surf, dive, and swim away

I wanted to drop my bucket and pail
Stomp flat the big sandcastle I built
Wave a man's good-bye to my mother
Who watched from under an umbrella

And plunge into the sea in his wake
As he disappeared under a green wave
And swam beyond the ropes and buoys
As if he would go on and on leaving me

Alone on the beach, bucket and pail,
Sandcastle fortified by moat and wall,
Ripples of tide washing my boy's feet
Sun suddenly warm on my shoulders

So I let my blue shovel drop into surf
Balled my small fists, bit my thin lip,
Curled my boy's toes, dug my heels,
Dabbed a sandy hand at my wet eye

Squinting to catch a glimpse of him
Now beyond waves and so far away
My man's sea-journey about to begin
Into the surf and under the deep sea

But my mother, behind sunglasses,
Called to me and I stayed on shore
Heeding her warning not to go deep
Watching my father swimming away

And now I still wonder what it's like
To go beyond the ropes and buoys
That keep me still standing on shore
And finally run, dive, and swim off

In my father's wake into the deep.

My Father, Past Eighty, On the Beach

He took long walks on the beach
Trailing behind his unleashed dog
Every morning after a short run
Praying with each step for each person

In his family, in the town, everyone
He ever met, even every stranger,
For their health and peace of mind
And their chance at a big break

The kind of big break, a better job,
A proposal from just the right one
The return of a prodigal once lost
Even an unexpected phone call

What he always wanted himself
But ended up helping others
To get. "Everybody deserves,"
He said, "their chance at bat."

As waves crashed beside his feet
Sometimes soaking him to ankles
And sun streaked across the surf
Like a long memory he kept close

He whispered his prayers to himself
Awash in the shore's warm sunlight
Breathing in every waft of salt air
Until he, surrounded by light, ascended.

The Rising

I always thought my father would fall
in the middle of a race, arms pumping,
eyes fixed on a finish line, chest heaving,
his big heart pounding out of his body

his spirit more than his feet bounding him
around Takanassee on a blue summer night
even as runners ahead flailed at the finish
pressing on, until the last step of all

or I always thought he would fall
in the middle of a swim, arms flashing
above the waves, legs thrashing
beyond the breakers and the buoys

his will more than his lifeguard's stroke
buoyant in turbulent tide
even as other swimmers flailed behind him
in stride, until the last gasp of all

but when I saw him fall, last heavy breath,
after a week of dying slowly in bed
I saw him again in the middle of a race
abounding under blue sky

And saw him again, far from shore,
beyond the lifeguard's ropes
in phosphorescence and moonlight
rising up, hand outstretched, free

When I Gave My Father's Eulogy

When I gave my father's eulogy
I heard the sound of waves

Rising up, spilling over the seawall
Roiling like a cloud up Beach Road

Splashing against the church door
A lone latecomer's loud knocking

Shuddering girders and rafters
Stirring the people in the pews

A high tide rising up to the altar
Where I stood, suddenly at sea,

Awed, inundated, and wondering
Which direction the tide would turn

If, in this darkness, we could see
How far we all are from any shore

If, surrounded, we ever could find
The way to the distant shore we seek

None ready yet for the final shore.
But instead I saw my father, finally

Ashore, I saw him again, after so long
Stranded, walking down the long beach

He loved, breaking again into a run
Picking up speed, the way he ran

That cold night when I followed him
The two of us searching for driftwood

On a cold beach when he disappeared
Into a distant mist of surf and clouds

At the end of the beach where tide
And rocks blocked the way ahead

On the beach he loved, no turning back
When I gave my father's eulogy.

In the Rehab Hospital

In a rehab hospital on Mother's Day
A young woman in a common room
recites a Rosary with two elderly ladies
In wheelchairs who mouth the words
before one nods off at Jesus' name
and all the praying abruptly stops,
while my mother, her leg in a cast
up to her knee, tells me a long story
about my father, who spent months
in this rehab hospital before he died,
and who whenever she was angry
could make her laugh so she quotes
Jay Leno: "You can't stay mad
at people who make you laugh."

At the train station on my way home,
a windy morning after a storm,
beside the track two little boys
play with toy trains in blossoms
plowing them through piles of pink
until one hears the train whistle
from far away, looks far ahead
down the track, and tells his father
"The train! The train is coming now!"
I wait behind to climb aboard,
knowing where this ride ends.

Sixty Feet Six Inches

Abner Doubleday invented perfection, my father always told me,
His chair up close, the Yankees at bat on TV, live or rebroadcast.

When he was sixteen, he hitchhiked from New Jersey to Florida
For a spring training tryout with the New York Baseball Giants.

Sixty feet six inches, pitcher's mound to home plate, the perfect
Distance for a perfect dual in the middle of a perfect diamond.

He watched Jackie Robinson's first game with the Montreal Royals
From bleachers in Jersey City's Roosevelt Stadium on April 18, 1946.

More than sixty feet six inches? The batter catches up to the fastball,
The curve doesn't curve over the plate. The changeup is batting practice.

In 1955, he was invited to spring training with the Pittsburgh Pirates,
A not-quite-good enough catcher with a not-quite-good enough arm.

Less than sixty feet six inches? The batter can't catch up to the fastball,
The curve doesn't curve over the plate. The slider doesn't slide enough.

He remembers a skinny rookie playing right field, a perfect ballplayer,
A whip for an arm, a basket for a glove, a gallop for a run, a deadly bat.

The baseball? 9 ¼ inches, perfect size, 5 ¼ ounces, perfect weight
For the curveball, the changeup, the slider, the fastball, the screwball.

Once during his spring with the Pirates, the shortstop late to the bag,
He double clutched his throw, the baserunner stealing second easily.

Perfect dimensions. How did Doubleday know the perfect distance?
Home to first, first to second, second to third, and third to home?

After he double clutched, a batboy delivered a slip of paper to home plate
From the general manager. The curt message? "Throw or go home. BR."

Doubleday's genius, he said, the game he invented is untimed, timeless
Yet every second, every inch, is perfectly timed, perfectly measured.

On his wedding night in Asbury Park, he stopped at the batting cages
On the boardwalk, swinging for it all, and never hit the ball better.

In what other sport is there even the possibility of a perfect game?
Don Larsen, he told me, an unlikely hero, perfect in a World Series.

Once when he met Bob Feller, both men well past their playing days,
He asked for a favor. "Just one pitch," he asked, and Feller delivered.

This perfect game of baseball, he liked to say so much, is a lot like life.
Get to the plate. Take your best swings. That's all you or anyone can do.

Babe Ruth walked back to the dugout after a game-winning home run,
He liked to say, exactly the same way he walked back after a strikeout.

Wrestling with Angels

They come into my bedroom, Angelo and Angela,
Talking trash, riling me up, usually in dreams.
"C'mon, dude, show us what you got!" That's Angelo,
Sleeves rolled up, sneering, ready for a fight.

I ignore them or try. "You," Angelo says, "I'm
Talking to you, buddy. Not Joshua. What the hell…"
They set on me, claws bared, beaks pecking, pecking,
Wings flapping, feathers flying, beady eyes popping…

They get me down, pinned against the bed sheets,
"Say uncle," says Angela. "Say goddamned uncle."
"No," Angelo says, "Say you'll go through with it.
You know, your destiny, and all that." "No,"

I say, but Angela's twisting my arm behind my back.
It's so hard wrestling with angels. They're a lot
Stronger than they look, and meaner, and smarter
Than you think. They're the better of me….and you.

The Bend in the Branch

In the bend in the branch
Over the edge of the pond

In stillness and silence
A whole October afternoon

Waits for wind or wave
An end of timelessness

To break the scene, split the silence
Topple the stillness, plunge

The branch, shatter mirrored
Water, steal a breath from me

Who listens in silence
For silence but hears its voice

On this edge of pond, its call
In the hum of nature

For me, the branch over the pond,
To break open, split, splinter, sunder

And fall, a splash in warm water,
And plunge, never to return

To my balancing act, the acrobatics
Of getting along, making it up, hanging in

Doing the expected next right thing
And instead sinking slowly, adrift,

The water enveloping me, my self
Swimming and breathing finally free.

My Horses

I haven't taken care of my horses.
Away from the barns, up at the house
In conversations with other people's lives
I've neglected them, left them to die.

When I remember I forgot my horses,
I run to the barn like remembering death.

Still alive in stalls, gaunt, mangy, feral
They nuzzle my empty hand as if to say,
Yes, we're here, we're always here,
Why have you been away so long?

What could be so important up at the house
That you left us alone so long to die?
We are your horses, your precious horses,
Where's your solemn vow to take care of us?

I'm haunted by what I have not done.
I haven't taken care of my horses.
In conversation with other people's lives
I forgot hay and water, ride and touch.

New Neighbors on North Park

New neighbors arrive on North Park
A family, skittish, alert for danger,
Standing, on uncut grass, stock-still,
Beside a house-for-sale sign.

I've seen them around, house-hunting,
Near vacant lots, abandoned properties
Wary at sheriff's sales, open houses,
Always looking for foreclosures.

They graze front lawns, flower gardens.
They stare. If I approach or even wave
They dart off, traipsing through backyards,
Or disappear into the woods.

Now I see they've taken up residence
On the front lawn of a North Park house
Across from the meadow and ravine
Integrating the neighborhood.

Nobody, they must say to themselves,
Lives here anymore. Why not us?
We won't make noise for the neighbors
And we'll keep the lawn, garden just so.

Shore of Home

I see now just how wrong I've been
about the shore I've longed for
looking for the wrong things

going the wrong way, too occupied
with measuring my shore by my heist.
For too long I've been a surfcaster

for myself, gearing up, tackle box, waders,
rod and line, bait, hoping for the big catch
lamenting the one that got away.

I should have left my gear at home
left my tokens of travel, mirrors
I looked into, removed my shoes,

hid them away under the lifeguard stand,
left my shirt, my preconceived ideas,
stripped down my thoughts about myself,

ones that cling like heavy clothing:
what I thought about heaven in childhood
what I feared about dying young

what I didn't see because I wasn't looking,
missing the turns in this odyssey, not wandering.
It has taken me so long, all these years,

to see it's not about going; it's about returning.
While you may be tempted to linger too long
with a Cyclops who doesn't know your name,

a Circe who waits tables in a seaside bar,
or a Nestor who drives a city cab at night,
your home's not Ithaca far from home,

an Ithaca isn't measured by steps or gains
but by how much you leave behind:
you will end the journey with nothing.

Only then, alone, will you find your father
who waits for you to tell you who you are,
And your son who waits for your footsteps,

And your love, besieged, now finally freed.

Grammar of Life

> *"Let him easter in us, be a dayspring to the dimness of us, be a crimson-cresseted east"*
> —*"Wreck of the Deutschland," Gerard Manley Hopkins*

It is grammatical, this life.
Rain rains. Snow snows.

Sun suns. Moon moons.
Root roots. Flower flowers.

Eye eyes. Finger fingers.
Dancer dances. Runner runs.

Mirror mirrors. Hope hopes.
Love loves. Hate hates.

So let singers sing. Prayers pray.
Let God god us.

Let Easter easter us,
grammatically, daily, everlastingly.

The Corner

for Margaret

When your hospital bed turned the corner
Into the other world of the operating room
I turned another corner out onto the street
Alone in a world I never saw before

Turning corner after corner after corner
Looking for something that hot afternoon
In store windows, in faces of passersby
In the empty blue sky, in the crawl of time

Because nothing remained of my world
In the two hours of your surgery while I waited
For the tsunami or the thunderstorm
Or the tornado or first light of a new morning

Under gray lights of a waiting room
Alone in a corner, cornered by love.

Flies and Fireflies

for my brothers

In our yard beside the shore
Before dark washed over us

After dinner and Italian ice
And our father's dugout stories

Late on long summer nights
Before school and football

We spun spinners at dusk
Twisted in pretzel swings

Chased high arcs of fly balls
We lost in the constellations

Leapt into outfield hedges
For long drives of wiffle balls

Raced barefoot around bases
Heading home in darkness

Lost track of the score
Base paths and foul lines

Until our hands on knees ready
Our father delivered the last pitch

To the surf's endless cheers
And fireflies' sudden applause

Hospice Down the Shore

Down the shore in the nursing home
beachcombers sit up in bed
sunbathers stop in wheelchairs
bennies, shoobies, snowbirds
who drove down the parkway
family station wagon packed
every summer Friday night
for rented weekend cottages
in Elberon, Barnegat, Bayside
who found monthly rentals
in Avon, Avalon, Atlantic City
whose children, grandchildren
now stash snapshots in boxes
of summer days long ago
big hair, sunglasses, flip-flops
crewcuts, Bermudas, loafers
strolling the endless strand
collecting mounds of shells
swimming out to breakers
bobbing in swells waving
watching under umbrellas
for children playing in surf
until the last light of summer.
Now hallway lights stay on
but inside darkened rooms
behind locked windows
they watch for first light
low waves on the shore
a path, any path, to the shore.

One Night, Not Alone

On the cinder path
Alone, not even the moon
Following me, I stopped
Halfway between streets

Listening for something
To remind me why I was
When a stooped, standoffish
Farmer in a three-piece suit

Joined me out of nowhere
Saying something about
A road less traveled.
I nodded a thank you.

Not sure of going on
I saw a precise woman
In an upstairs room
Dwelling in possibilities

And at the next corner
A cosmos, one of the roughs,
Loosed a barbaric yawp
And a password primeval.

Still in the dark I met
A slim, world-weary man
Whispering about finding
Beginnings in endings

And behind him, hidden,
A squat bald man shouted
About the best minds
Of his generation lost

And left me alone again
On the moonless path
Still walking alone
Listening for something

Until I heard a crowd
under a streetlight
their voices like songs
telling their stories

turning a widening gyre
raging at the dying light
living in a pretty how town
eating men like air

lying in a hammock
looking at a blackbird
digging in the peat
stopping all the clocks

eating all the plums
dreaming a dream deferred
mastering the art of losing
breaking into blossom

diving into a wreck
taking waking slow
jazzing June. We
traveling through the dark

and stood on the edge
under shadow of night
and joined, off-key,
their songs of light.

Milton Keynes UK
Ingram Content Group UK Ltd.
UKHW040255291024
450401UK00006B/51